LLC for Beginners

The Most Resourced Guide on How to Begin, Grow and Get the Most Out of Your LLC

Nigel Stephens

TABLE OF CONTENTS

INTRODUCTION

You only have to do a few things right in your life so long as you don t do too many things wrong.
—Warren Buffett

Like every other kind of business out there, a Limited Liability Company (LLC) has its own set of associated advantages and disadvantages. In recent years, LLCs have become increasingly common and are currently a viable long-term option, especially for small businesses and new companies that do not have streamlined revenue streams. The biggest reason behind this is obviously the level of protection that LLCs provide to all their members with respect to private assets. LLCs are easier to form than corporations, might have various tax benefits, and eliminate a range of complications associated with the formation and management of a company.

On the other hand, there are a range of questions that need to be answered before a business is converted into an LLC. As far as taxation is concerned, LLCs are generally considered partnerships, which means that the revenue accrued by members who work for the business will be considered self-employment, and generally attract a higher rate of interest. This is one problem that can be solved by simply opting to be taxed as a corporation, which will enable the members to be taxed only on the compensation that they derive and not the pre-tax income that is generated by the LLC. Furthermore, while LLCs provide increased protection for all members, including investors, the amount of control that each member exerts might be limited. One such example is that if an owner decides to leave the company due to any reason, the LLC will need to be dissolved and the other owners will have to form another LLC to continue being in business.

Still, there is little doubt that operating as an LLC can prove extremely beneficial for small and medium-sized companies. In a nutshell, they allow business owners to combine the benefits of a corporation with those of a limited liability partnership or a sole proprietorship. As a new business owner attempts to scale up and establish themselves in their chosen sector, a range of known and unknown challenges are bound to crop up. These may tend to drive up costs, reduce sales, or, like the COVID pandemic, curtail the market in a variety of ways. According to the US government, exactly 61.7 percent of companies with employees requested for financial assistance from the Paycheck Protection Program (PPP) as a result of the losses incurred in 2020 alone due to the pandemic. Financial assistance was provided to 58.3% of all companies during the financial year.

As far as retail trade was concerned, the numbers were even higher and more alarming. 69.9% of the total companies with employees in the retail sector asked for financial assistance under the PPP in 2020, which was received by 66.3% of them. Furthermore, financial assistance from the Small Business Administration Forgiveness Loan program was requested by 21% of the total companies with employees and received by 16.3% of them. (Bureau, n.d.)

Moving on, an overall 62.8% of total companies with employees received financial assistance of some sort from the US government as a result of the COVID pandemic. While the pandemic undoubtedly presented a slew of challenges that many small businesses were simply unprepared to face, a number of larger corporations also faced insolvency, especially those in sectors dependent upon consumer spendings. According to an S&P Global Market Intelligence analysis, a total of 630 companies filed for bankruptcy in the US in 2020 alone. (US Corporate Bankruptcies End 2020 at a 10-Year High amid the COVID-19 Pandemic, n.d.)

Some of the bigger companies that turned bankrupt include Neiman Marcus Group Inc., J. C. Penney Co. Inc., Ascena Retail Group Inc., Tailored Brands Inc., Fieldwood Energy Inc., and Chesapeake Energy Corp. The analysis was only limited to the companies that had an overall value, in the form of liabilities or assets, of at least $2 million. The situation has surely improved in recent months, and consumer spending is increasing again. However, common sense stipulates that the brunt of the burden has been borne by smaller businesses, and the result is there for all to see. A range of established small businesses have been forced to close, and the overall number of bankruptcy filings was the highest since 2010.

Even the companies that were able to stay afloat registered large-scale losses and were forced to scale down. The fact is that several reasons can contribute to a business not succeeding. While some may be due to avoidable circumstances, others might be out of the owners 'control. Forming an LLC is the easiest way in which members can give themselves and their personal assets a high level of protection, as the assets and liabilities of the company are considered separate from those of the individuals. Like every big business decision, the decision to form an LLC is also one that must be taken after doing the right research. Owners should spend the right amount of time determining the kinds of benefits and disadvantages that will result from the conversion to an LLC.

Quite often, the stage of a business will play a significant role in determining whether it is the right time to form an LLC. Corporation owners are personally liable for the liabilities of the company if it goes bankrupt. Established companies that have consistent revenue will not be worried about such events, and the company is also bound to have more assets in order to take care of its liabilities.

An LLC has a lot of similarities with corporations, with the major difference lying in the way that they are taxed. The availability of this "flow-through" taxation, which happens on an individual basis, is a feature that LLCs derive from partnerships. LLCs are therefore hybrid entities that combine the features of a corporation with those of a partnership, allowing smaller businesses to maintain a higher level of protection for the personal assets of their owners.

The following writeup has been written with the aim of educating business owners who are considering or have decided to convert their companies into LLCs. The writeup aims to provide all the information that business owners require with respect to the nature of LLCs, how they might benefit the business in question, and the various laws and requirements that govern the ability of a company to be converted into an LLC. Starting off with the basics, the book will move on to specific advice and tips that business owners can make use of and avoid common mistakes that business owners tend to make at this stage of their journey. Apart from pointed advice, the book can also be seen as a source of education for business enthusiasts and others who wish to understand the nature, features, requirements, and other factors that go behind the creation of a successful LLC.

CHAPTER 1: BEING AN ENTREPRENEUR—WHAT IS IT ABOUT?

As mentioned before, LLCs are hybrid entities that combine features of a corporation with those of a partnership or a sole proprietorship. The primary feature that distinguishes an LLC from other types of corporations is thus the protection it provides owners regarding their personal assets in relation to the company's overall liabilities and debts. The kind of laws and regulations that will govern LLCs and their formulation tend to vary from state to state, especially in the US.

Furthermore, while anybody can convert their business to an LLC generally, there are certain parties that are not allowed to be members. This generally includes banks, insurance companies, and other financial organizations, as the possibility of bankruptcy in these situations is much higher than that in the retail sector. Hence, the level of protection towards personal assets by LLCs is considered unfair for these organizations.

Moving on, another basic feature of an LLC is that it is not taxed directly. As mentioned previously, LLCs undergo what is known as "flow-through" taxation. This means that instead of the organization being directly taxed for the earnings, the earnings travel to the members, who are then expected to declare them as part of their tax returns. This means that LLCs are taxed through individual tax returns rather than the organization being taxed on its overall earnings.

As far as state laws are concerned, they tend to show quite a bit of variance when it comes to LLCs. Different states have different kinds of laws and regulations, and owners are referred to as "members." Moreover, LLCs are permitted under specific state statutes, and there are no specific central laws that apply to their governance. While some states tend to restrict ownership, most don't. This means that LLCs provide an interesting option for investment for a range of parties, including individuals, corporations, foreigners, foreign entities, and even other LLCs. However, financial institutions such as banks are not generally allowed to be members.

Due to the nature of taxation afforded to LLCs, they provide a viable option for business owners who want to protect their personal assets but do not yet have dependable sources of streamlined income. While LLCs are given the option to stick to this system of "flow-through" taxation, members can also opt to be taxed like corporations. This means that rather than the tax being deducted as individual tax returns, it will be directly deducted from the company's earnings in that particular financial year.

While this may still prove useful, as members will still get the same kind of protection, there are various instances where the courts might allow people to sue the members for the liabilities of the company. This is true with respect to fraud or if the LLC in question has failed to meet its reporting or legal requirements.

The fact is that, as an entrepreneur, it is the owner's responsibility to weigh the pros and cons of a potential conversion into an LLC. Sometimes, entrepreneurship is simply about knowing the right information rather than taking too many initiatives. Conversion into an LLC can open the company up to a range of benefits, and people might need to research various aspects in order to determine the extent of benefits that they can accrue.

Once the decision has been made, the owner will then need to investigate the various requirements that they need to fulfill with respect to the actual formation of the LLC.

Basics of Forming an LLC

First and foremost, owners or members will need to choose a specific name for the company. This task might already have been taken care of, especially if the company has already been in business for a certain period. While the requirements that need to be fulfilled in different US states with respect to the formation of an LLC might vary, there are various basic commonalities that need to be taken care of.

Every LLC needs to create Articles of Organization that can be documented and registered with the state. The Articles of Organization determine all the rules and regulations that will govern the various members of the LLC. For example, the articles of organization establish the various rights, powers, duties, liabilities, and obligations placed on each member of the LLC. Furthermore, the contact information of the various LLC members, including their names and addresses, the name of the LLC's registered agent(s), and the statement of purpose of the business are generally included in the articles of organization.

These articles basically determine the various basic features of the LLC and govern the kinds of responsibilities and liabilities that every member must fulfill. Along with the filing of the articles of organization, the LLC also must pay a fee to the state at the time of conversion. While no federal laws directly apply to the taxation or the governance of LLCs, the companies do have to pay a fee at the federal level in order to obtain an Employer Identification Number (EIN). As a matter of fact, every business entity operating in the US must obtain an EIN in order to register itself.

In themselves, LLCs are hybrid entities that combine the limited liability features of a corporation with the taxation and management flexibility of a partnership. A corporation has various liability protections, which means that only in special circumstances are people allowed to sue owners for the liabilities of the company. However, unlike corporations that are allowed to exist in perpetuity, LLCs are dissolved when the company goes bankrupt or one of the members leaves or dies. This means that forming an LLC is not a viable option for business owners who plan to convert the business into a public company in the future.

A partnership can also be viewed as a business agreement between two or more parties. LLCs differ from partnerships regarding the protection available with respect to personal assets. However, both entities are allowed to pass their profits through their employees, who then pay tax based on their individual tax returns. The losses can be used to offset other income, but only until the amount of money invested increases. This means that LLC owners have two options with respect to taxation.

By filing Form 1065, they can opt to be taxed like a partnership, and by filing Form 1120, the company can opt to be taxed like a corporation. (Kenton, 2021) In order to protect the LLC against closure due to the death of one of the members, a business continuation agreement must be in place. Without it, the LLC will be dissolved at the death of any of the members. Entrepreneurs should consider the two outlined benefits that LLCs can potentially provide and whether they can prove to be a game changer for the overall business:

- Members will not be personally liable, and their personal assets will be protected if the company goes bankrupt or is sued.

- Members will be taxed individually, which means that double taxation will be avoided. Normally, not only are the employees taxed separately according to their income, but the company is also taxed for its income. Forming an LLC can allow the business to pass its profits to the members, which will avoid double taxation.

Of course, while LLCs, especially in the US, are generally preferred by smaller businesses, plenty of bigger companies are also in fact LLCs. This includes Alphabet, which is the parent company of Google, PepsiCo Inc., Exxon Mobil Corp., and Johnson & Johnson. Smaller forms of LLCs include family LLCs, sole proprietorship LLCs, and member-managed LLCs. Various medical practitioners, such as physicians, also prefer to register as an LLC rather than a company or a partnership. For medical practitioners, forming an LLC can prove to be extremely useful and protect them against various malpractice-related suits. In this way, what LLCs effectively do is combine some key features of a corporation with those of a partnership. Corporations are exposed to double taxation, which LLCs have the option to avoid. LLCs also provide flexibility in management and governance, which corporations do not have.

Finally, unlike partnerships, members of an LLC have the same kind of protection for personal assets as corporation owners get. While certain sectors and bigger companies might prefer to function as corporations sometimes due to their sheer size, the advantages associated with LLCs have made them the most common forms of business entities in the US. As of 2004, there were roughly 21.6 million LLCs in the US, with a total of 23.6 million sole proprietary businesses, and only 1.6 million registered corporations. (Is It Time to Think about an LLC for Your Business? | Fitzpatrick Lentz & Bubba, n.d.) According to the IRS, the number of LLCs has shown a yearly increase since 2004 which also points towards the various advantages that LLC members can accrue from the conversion. (SOI Tax Stats - Partnership Statistics by Entity Type | Internal Revenue Service, n.d.)

Chapter 2: LLCs and Other Businesses—A Comparison

There are various things to consider before starting a business. The kind of business structure that one chooses will influence a range of everyday processes that the business is involved in. This includes the kind and level of taxation, the personal liability, and the everyday operations that the business must conduct. Choosing the right balance of legal protections and benefits is paramount to the success of the business. Before registering the business with a specific state, owners will need to choose a specific business structure. There are quite a few options to choose from.

Furthermore, it is possible to change to a different business structure in the future. However, specific states might have various restrictions with respect to such a conversion, which is another factor that needs to be investigated during this stage. While consulting with a business specialist to understand how specific structures might benefit the company in question might prove useful, the following sections are aimed at providing a basic set of guidelines that can help entrepreneurs make this all-important decision with respect to their business structure.

Sole Proprietorship

A sole proprietorship is easily the most straightforward business structure and gives the owners the highest amount of control possible over their business. Every owner who does not register themselves as a business entity is automatically considered a sole proprietor, which means that it is straightforward to become a sole proprietor. Being a sole proprietor does not create another business entity. Instead, the income, assets, and liabilities of the individual are not separate from those of the sole proprietorship.

This means that if a case is filed or the business is sued for liabilities, the other party will be able to personally file charges against the business owner and have a right to their personal assets. While this gives a large amount of control to the owner with respect to various business decisions, problems can arise as well. This is true with respect to raising money, as banks are reluctant to lend to sole proprietors, and there is no option of selling stock as well. However, owners still get to choose a trade name that they can use. As there is little to no protection given towards personal assets, a sole proprietorship is generally a good option for owners who have not yet formally started a business and only want to test their idea on a limited scale. Newer businesses tend to start off as sole proprietorships, although these businesses have the option of choosing another business structure later.

Partnerships

A partnership is the easiest way in which two or more people can be part owners of a business. US law allows for the creation of two kinds of partnerships: limited partnership and limited liability partnerships. A limited partnership will have one general owner who will have unlimited liability, and his personal assets may be at risk if a suit against the business is filed. At the same time, all other partners in the business will have limited liability.

These partners also tend to have less control over the business, which is stipulated in the partnership agreement that the parties enter.

The general partner is also expected to pay the taxes as part of their personal tax returns, as well as self-employment rates. On the other hand, a limited liability partnership will have multiple owners who all have limited liabilities. This means that their personal assets will be protected with respect to the debts and liabilities of the company. Furthermore, individual partners will not be liable for the actions of other partners, in which case personal assets will be at risk.

Partnerships have traditionally been seen as a popular option for groups of professionals such as attorneys and medical professionals. On the other hand, partnerships also tend to be the ideal option for businesses with multiple owners, as well as for owners who are still in the initial stage of testing out their business ideas. Partnerships are also a common business structure that might be more suitable for certain business types.

Limited Liability Company

The most common form of business structure out there, an LLC, or a Limited Liability Company, effectively combines the features of a partnership with those of a company. Business owners can benefit from the advantages accrued from both the partnership and sole proprietorship business structures by opting for an LLC. One of the most important questions to address when choosing a business structure is what kind of protection towards personal assets must be provided as part of the structure.

An LLC protects the personal assets of owners by making them separate from the company's assets. This means that at the time a case is filed for the payment of liabilities, the personal assets of the owner will be safe, and it is the company that will be affected. If there has been no crime related to fraud or other acts by the individual owner, the LLC will be directly liable in the event of a lawsuit or bankruptcy.

By default, members of an LLC must pay corporate taxes as part of their individual tax returns and other charges that might be applicable, related to healthcare and social security. Furthermore, while certain states require LLCs to be dissolved at the death of a member, there are options that can avoid this possibility. For example, a pre-existing trade agreement that allows the LLC to operate even after one or more member's leave is a possibility. This agreement can also be related to the transfer of ownership, implying that LLCs need not be a short-term structure.

This means that the type of business structure that should be chosen must be determined by the intentions and expectations of the business owners. Different structures provide various types of benefits. However, for smaller businesses, LLCs tend to combine the best features of a corporation with those of a partnership. For owners who operate medium- to high-risk businesses that are dependent upon external factors for their success, LLCs can prove to be the ideal choice. This is also true for business owners who are just starting out and want to gauge the level of success that is possible in their chosen industry.

In terms of corporations, most bigger businesses prefer to be corporations simply because of the level of protection they provide to business owners in terms of their personal assets. However, both S-corporations and C-corporations have specific disadvantages when compared with an LLC. A C-corporation undergoes double taxation. This first happens at the company level, and the individual employees also end up paying income tax as part of their individual ITRs. S-corporations, on the other hand, do not allow the same kind of control with respect to ownership as LLCs do. The process to start and operate an LLC is straightforward, has fewer formalities than other structures, has greater flexibility, and has limited liability for owners.

Hence, while corporations are the common aim of bigger companies, LLCs offer a range of advantages that simply make them better suited for newer businesses. Especially towards the beginning, owners need limited liability in terms of personal assets. This protects them from various possibilities. If the business fails to take off and there are bankruptcy or liability-related suits that are filed, the personal assets of members will be protected. Hence, in simple terms, LLCs combine the simplicity, flexibility, and various taxation-related benefits of different structures.

Now, it must be remembered that this protection that LLCs give is not applicable in all kinds of situations. In certain cases where the member has committed a crime, or fraud, their personal assets will also be at risk if a suit is filed related to their personal actions. However, in the simple case of the LLC not being able to pay off its liabilities, the member will not be personally liable. Of course, the flexibility that LLCs lend is also related to the kind of entity it is registered as, as far as taxation is concerned. An LLC can take on the tax status of a corporation and a sole proprietorship. These other structures also have a range of requirements related to filing and registration. In terms of various organizational and other types of formalities, LLCs have a more straightforward process.

Moving on, the management-related flexibility that LLCs provide is also related to the operating agreement that the company creates. The agreement is simple to change and introduce changes to. There are two types of management structures available to LLCs. A "member-managed" LLC requires members to act as the decision makers of the company. In a "manager-managed" LLC, members need to choose various managers to run specific parts of the business or the entire business itself.

The operating agreement also specifies the various processes that go on behind a member vote. In most states, voting power is per capita. This means that each member gets a single vote. However, the LLC can also choose to distribute voting power in accordance with the capital contribution by simply stipulating it in the operating agreement. Other advantages might be specific in nature. For example, in the case of an S-corporation, foreign shareholders, corporations, and having more than a hundred shareholders are not allowed. Furthermore, corporations also have other requirements related to the business structure and the board of directors. In the case of an LLC, these requirements do not exist.

This means that LLCs, in addition to combining the advantages of a range of business structures, also deliver specific benefits to various business owners that are simply not possible to derive from other structures.

CHAPTER 3: HOW TO CREATE AN LLC?

The sections until now dealt with the range of benefits that business owners can derive from an LLC. However, the method of forming an LLC can prove to be a challenge, especially with respect to different states in the US. As mentioned before, an LLC is a separate legal entity. This basically means that the personal assets and liabilities of the company are separate from those of the members. Hence, an LLC protects members and their personal assets in the case of lawsuits related to the liabilities of the company.

At the same time, various cases might result in the members being sued separately. This happens when the member commits a crime or defrauds the shareholders or other members of the LLC. Being a separate legal entity also means that the LLC is protected in case one or more members end up leaving. This would mean that the members who leave will have no claim over the personal assets of the company, thereby allowing the company to exist and thrive. Moreover, while LLCs in themselves can be sued, the members of the company end up protected, unless a crime has been committed.

As far as the formation of an LLC is concerned, specific steps need to be followed, and the organization also needs to be registered with the state in question. First and foremost, while most business owners might be focused on doing business, the business name needs to be chosen and registered with the state. Most states do not allow companies to use names that are already being used by other LLCs. Furthermore, states might also discourage the use of various words that signify that the company is related to specific industries, such as insurance or banking. Individual states might also have laws stipulating the inclusion of the term "LLC" in the name of the business.

In order to create an LLC, the first step is therefore to choose a name and then get it registered with the state in which the LLC wants to conduct its business. Moving on, the next thing that must be done in order to convert into an LLC is the employment of a registered agent. While most LLCs will have at least one employee who can be the registered agent, there are various companies and services that can be used in order to create a registered agent for the company in question. This means that various registered agents do not need to be employees of the LLC in question. This is useful for foreign members or LLCs that want to conduct at least some part of their business in the US. Foreign LLCs will be able to easily allot a registered agent who needs to be present at an office during working hours in the state in which the LLC is registered. Apart from a stipulated need to have a registered agent, they are also responsible for the communication and the receiving of official and legal documents related to the LLC. The registered agent is simply the means by which various legal and official communications are made with the LLC. The agent is expected to turn in the documents to the member of the LLC who is in charge after receiving all documents.

Once this is done, the LLC will be ready to be registered. To do that, the owner must get a copy of the LLC article of organization form of the state in which the LLC is to be registered. As mentioned before, it is the article of organization that determines a range of important information as far as the company is concerned. Some US states use the term "certificate of formation" instead of "an article of organization." Regardless, each state will have a form that will need to be downloaded from the website and then filled in. At the very least, the article of organization will include the following basic information about the LLC:

- the name of the business

- the address of the principal place of business

- the stated purpose of the business

- information regarding the management of the LLC

- information about the registered agent, as well as a signed document from the agent

- the overall time period or duration of the LLC

As mentioned before, the article of organization can have a range of other information that is deemed important for conducting business. This includes information related to what happens when one of the members ends up leaving or dies. In most states, the LLC is expected to be dissolved when such an event takes place. There are two solutions available for an LLC to solve this situation. The article of organization can have a statute allowing the LLC to conduct its business even after one of the members leaves. If such a statute is not added, the LLC will need to be dissolved and another one will need to be registered if the other members want to continue being in business. In most states, it is the secretary of state's website that has all the information required to form an LLC.

The article of organization also needs to be signed by one or all the members. During this time, various states such as New York and Nebraska also stipulate the requirement of the publication of a newspaper notice indicating the owners 'desire to form the LLC.

At the time of filing the articles of organization, the members need to pay a fee to the state. This fee varies in different states and is generally called the filing fee. If the LLC can fulfill all requirements and there are no issues with the article of organization, the LLC will be registered quickly, and the specific state will issue a certificate indicating that the LLC has been registered. Finally, this registration certificate allows the members to fulfill various other important commitments that need to be completed for the LLC to function. This includes the setting up of a business account as well as the tax ID number, which is required especially in case the LLC has opted to be taxed like a corporation. Every LLC gets a tax ID number, and these documents are also expected to be produced if the members decide to change their business structure in the future.

Once the article of organization has been approved and the certificate issued, members can focus on the creation of the operating agreement. While the article on organization deals with various basic features of the LLC, the operating agreement contains information regarding all the important decision-making processes for the LLC. As mentioned before, the operating agreement includes all the legal, management, and financial rights of various members of the LLC. There are two types of LLCs: member-managed and manager-managed. It is the operating agreement that determines the nature of the LLC and the various processes that will need to be followed with respect to all the decision-making of the company.

The operating agreement forms the crux of the LLC. It determines who will bear the capital burden and how the profits will be distributed among the employees. It also stipulates the method by which specific members are allowed to leave the LLC. By understanding the various natures and the semantics of the business, every member can get a basic understanding of their roles, responsibilities, and burdens, as well as the kind of personal protection that will be afforded to them. The operating agreement also determines which employee controls what part of the business. While these agreements are especially important for LLCs that include more than one member, they can be just as crucial for LLCs with single members. Furthermore, the creation of an operating agreement has been made straightforward and free due to the existence of various websites that offer precise templates that companies can follow.

The aim of the operating agreement is to tailor the various stipulations and methods that the LLC will follow with respect to all kinds of commitments and functions. An operating agreement can help owners create ideal systems that can help them grow and operate, and it must be filed before the actual business commences.

Once the operating agreement has been created, the LLC is ready to be active. The business can then move on to subsequent marketing and profit-creating activities that will help it establish itself. While the above steps are all the information an owner needs in order to correctly register their LLC, there are various other subsequent legal requirements that may need to be fulfilled as well.

For example, various states require LLCs to submit annual statements and reveal other information that might be asked for on the state secretary's website. Furthermore, an annual fee might also need to be paid. Other requirements that the LLC needs to fulfill might also be added regularly to the website. The owners need to regularly check these updates in order to ensure that their LLC is in good standing with the state. This ensures that no subsequent problems come up once the LLC actively begins business.

CHAPTER 4: THE TAXATION OF AN LLC

As mentioned, several times, an LLC can choose to be taxed as a corporation or as a partnership. While most states do not restrict ownership of an LLC, some do. Most states also allow single-member LLCs to be formed. In such a scenario, the LLC can be taxed as a separate entity, or the individual owner can pay taxes as part of their own tax returns. However, when the LLC chooses to be taxed like a partnership, i.e., as part of individual tax returns, double taxation is avoided.

The IRS treats LLCs as either a corporation or a partnership. (IRS, 2019) Furthermore, in the case of single-member LLCs, the IRS automatically treats them like a partnership. This means that the individual will be taxed separately, and the LLC will not be treated as a special legal entity of its own. However, if the single-member LLC opts to file Form 8832, it is then treated as a corporation, and the LLC is a separate entity that exposes the owner to double taxation.

This kind of flexibility is what has made LLCs so common and one of the most obvious choices for newer businesses that are still trying to establish themselves. In the case of corporations, while there is a lot of protection afforded to the personal assets of members, this flexibility with respect to management and decision-making is simply not possible. Furthermore, while corporations expose the business to double taxation, this is also avoidable in the case of LLCs, as they can opt to be taxed like a partnership. There is little doubt that the mode of taxation is one of the most important considerations to choose from as far as a business structure is concerned.

For federal tax purposes, LLCs are typically treated as pass-through structures. This means that the company in question does not directly pay taxes out of its business income. Instead, members of the LLC pay taxes out of their individual shares of the LLC's profits. This is exactly how a partnership, or a sole proprietorship is taxed. Apart from the tax on the income derived from the LLC, individuals also end up paying self-employment taxes. Other taxes that they might be expected to pay might be related to payroll and sales taxes applicable to the products of the LLC.

Of course, as mentioned several times, the LLC also has the option of being taxed like a corporation. As far as single-member LLCs are concerned, they are regarded as sole proprietorships by the federal government, and the tax system described above is applicable. The same is true for multi-member LLCs. Here, as there are a range of members who all need to be taxed, the taxation is done based on individual incomes, but the effective system is still similar to that of a partnership. Things can quickly get complicated if the LLC chooses to be taxed like a corporation. If the LLC chooses to be treated as a C-corporation, the taxes will be filed by filing Form 8832 with the IRS. The LLC will be subject to a 21% federal corporate tax rate, and Form 1120 will also need to be filed with the federal government. (Prakash, 2020)

Moving on, an S-corporation will need to file Form 2553 with the IRS. It will be accompanied by the filing of Form 1120S. Of course, this taxation system is still incomplete, and LLCs also need to pay other taxes and fees to the state government. These include various unemployment taxes, social security, and Medicare-related expenses that also need to be taxed. These additional taxes can be as high as 15.3% of the overall income:

- 12.4% social security tax on earnings up to $137,700
- 2.9% Medicare tax on all earnings
- 0.9% Medicare surtax on earnings over $200,000 (Prakash, 2020).

CHAPTER 5: THE ORGANIZATIONAL STATE OF LLCS

The Limited Liability Company Act was created in 1996 and underwent major revisions in 2006. (Limited Liability Company Act, Revised - Uniform Law Commission, n.d.) As mentioned before, in order to be registered, LLCs need to file articles of organization with the respective state authorities. It is only upon the approval of these articles that the LLC will be considered a separate legal and business entity for tax purposes. As mentioned before, each state generally charges a one-time fee in order to be initially registered. While there are other mandatory filings that need to be taken care of at regular intervals, it is the initial registration that allows the LLC to function in the respective state.

As mentioned in the relevant section, the registration can be done by a foreign LLC as well. However, a registered agent will need to be hired who will act as the intermediary for all legal and other official communications. As far as the actual organization and functioning of the LLC are concerned, it is the articles of organization that determine each aspect with respect to the powers, duties, and the procedure that needs to be followed if a member ends up leaving for any reason. At the very least, the following information is mandatory to be filed as part of the articles of organization by the LLC:

- The name of the company.

- Names and contact information of all the founding members.

- The actual address of the business.

- The purpose and extent of the business.

- The name and contact information of the registered agent.

- The name of all the managers and the directors employed by the LLC.

- The date at which the LLC officially starts business.

- The overall duration of the LLC.

The above information is considered basic for all LLCs and must be included in the articles of organization. In this way, the articles of organization are like what are known as the articles of incorporation for companies and can also be known as a "certificate of organization" or "certificate of formation." The provisions and articles constitute the identity and nature of the LLC. They create the rights, powers, duties, obligations, and other liabilities that exist between the LLC and its members, as well as between the members of the LLC.

While filing procedures might vary from state to state, articles of organization are sometimes referred to as articles of association in countries other than the US. As far as the US is concerned, many cities and counties might have specific requirements related to licensing and zoning. There might also be extra fees associated with these requirements. Furthermore, as some industries are more heavily regulated than others, the nature of the LLC might also result in some extra requirements that need to be completed. These might be related to information that is expected to be included in the articles of organization. In the state of New York, LLCs are expected to file their operating agreements within 90 days of filing their articles of organization. (Hussain, 2022) While the process has been made straightforward in most states, many LLCs choose to hire a lawyer who can assist them through it. The registered articles of organization serve as the legal basis, or identity, of the LLC. It is the document that gives it its special identity and allows it to function as a registered business entity.

How to File Articles of Organization?

As mentioned before, the process itself is straightforward in most states, and generally begins on the website of the Secretary of State. The website will have all the information as well as the cost of filing the articles of organization.

Once the information has been gathered, the form must be filed correctly, and all the necessary information must be included. The process generally requires the answering of various questions that will be related to the purpose of the LLC, as well as personal information about the manager and the members of the company.

Most states offer the option of submitting forms both online and via regular mail. Even after the filing of the form, there are various steps that need to be completed. This includes obtaining an EIN, or an employer identification number. The EIN allows the LLC to open a business banking account, get a business license, and file taxes for the business in question.

Finally, while having an operating agreement is not compulsory, most LLCs prefer to have one to ensure flexibility and efficiency in the daily decision-making of the business. Again, this can be done on the website of the

Secretary of State. This step will be followed by the opening of a business bank account, which is also a straightforward process in the US. Finally, all the above documents will be necessary to obtain a business license, which will require the LLC to fulfill various requirements of the state. Apart from a state license, a federal license might also be required depending on the nature of the LLC.

In themselves, the articles of organization therefore form the basis of the identity of the LLC. It stipulates information related to various members, their relationships, and their responsibilities as far as the LLC is concerned. It also stipulates the various processes related to decision-making and the procedure to follow in case one of the members ends up leaving. In a nutshell, the articles of organization are the most important piece of documentation for the LLC and allow it to function, be taxed, and exist as a separate business entity.

Chapter 6: The Operating Agreement—How Does it Function?

While the Articles of Organization form the basis of the identity of the LLC, the operating agreement is more related to its functioning and the daily decision-making of the LLC. In themselves, the various statutes and the state law of the respective state decide what kind of information and statutes need to be included in the articles of organization. However, the operating agreement allows members to add their own customizations with respect to the workings of the LLC. Just like the articles of incorporation stipulate the various financial and decision-making information of the company, the operating agreement also acts in a similar manner for an LLC. In this way, articles of incorporation are essentially a combination of the operating agreement and the articles of organization, as far as a corporation is concerned.

The specific needs and detailed information about the functioning of the LLC are generally included in the operating agreement. As mentioned before, most states do not require an LLC to file an operating agreement. However, operating agreements lend a sense of efficiency and allow for the smooth running of the LLC. The operating agreement specifies the processes and people in charge of most the LLC's daily and critical decisions.

The operating agreement, once created, needs to be signed by each member of the LLC. This is because the operating agreement acts as a binding set of rules for the members that must be adhered to. Not doing so can lead to consequences and might even lead to the expulsion of the member in question. The operating agreement generally also includes information regarding how the LLC will react if one or more of its members fail to complete their responsibilities as stipulated in the operating agreement. The agreement is therefore essentially drafted to allow the senior members to decide how the LLC will function and to provide information about the various internal operations of the company.

In a nutshell, most states do not compulsorily stipulate the requirement of an operating agreement. However, in order to make full use of the special hybrid entity that is an LLC, having an operating agreement is generally considered ideal. In certain states, such as Missouri, California, and New York, the operating agreement is a requirement during the registration process. However, in most other states, they are merely an option, but the extra flexibility and the ability to customize the internal affairs as well as the decision-making of the company means that they can prove to be extremely useful.

Not having an operating agreement means that the LLC will have to adhere to the default rules of the state. These rules can cause a range of problems. For example, some states stipulate that the profits will be distributed equally among the members of the LLC, regardless of their capital contribution. In such a scenario, having an operating agreement will allow the members to take control over the distribution of profits from the LLC. If the LLC is operating as a sole proprietorship or partnership, there will be personal liability if the operating agreement does not stipulate that the members are protected if any suit or liability arises with respect to the LLC. Therefore, having an operating agreement can also protect members in case the LLC goes bankrupt.

The operating agreement allows the LLC to decide the rules related to voting and various meetings, as well as the procedure to be followed in case of succession or resignation. Most states stipulate that the following information must be included in an operating agreement, if filed:

- ownership status and percentage of each member
- responsibilities and rights of each member
- duties and powers of each member
- the profit allocation between members
- information related to the management and decision making of the LLC
- information regarding voting and meetings
- buyout and buy-sell provisions, as well as information about how the LLC will react when members wish to leave or sell

Furthermore, the operating agreement also spells out information related to various basic stipulations, how long the LLC will exist, and where it is located. As mentioned before, in the absence of an operating agreement, LLCs will be subjected to the default rules and regulations of the state in question. There is little doubt that these regulations are bound to fall short in various cases, depending upon the nature and functioning of the LLC. It is the operating agreement that allows the LLC to escape these basic rules and have their own customization regarding the needs of various members.

Finally, operating agreements also lend a sense of flexibility to the LLC. They are not permanent in nature, and the method of amendment is generally provided for in the agreement itself. Various stipulations regarding the voting share required of the LLC or the specific period in which amendments will be allowed can also be included in the operating agreement. If the process of amendment is not clearly stated in the operating agreement, the default rules will apply, and the state law will determine how the operating agreement can be amended. Some LLCs might also have an operating agreement that cannot be amended, which again stipulated the agreement.

Therefore, the operating agreement is another crucial document that allows the LLC to function effectively and efficiently. It determines various customizations that members might need or want with respect to the running of the LLC. As LLCs have a special hybrid structure, they allow a range of flexibilities and benefits that can be made use of, especially when an efficient operating agreement is in existence.

CHAPTER 7: HOW TO CONVERT AN EXISTING BUSINESS INTO AN LLC?

Considering the tax advantages and the management flexibility that LLCs provide, there are various benefits that can be accrued by converting an existing business into an LLC. As far as the conversion of a corporation is concerned, most states offer a streamlined process that allows the corporation to be directly converted into an LLC. The lack of a streamlined process means that the corporation will need to be dissolved and a new LLC will need to be registered for the effective conversion to happen.

Such a streamlined conversion is usually the most cost-effective and straightforward way in which a corporation can be converted into an LLC. Another option available to corporations is the merger option, which allows the corporation to create a merger agreement aimed at the transfer of ownership rights from shares to membership units. In this method, corporations will need to dissolve themselves in accordance with the rules of the specific state and create a new LLC, becoming a separate business entity.

Finally, the third method of conversion available to corporations is the traditional conversion. Every state allows corporations to fill out specific forms that allow the corporation to be converted into an LLC. This leads to the dissolution of the corporation status of the company and the creation of a new LLC. As mentioned before, there are a range of advantages that LLCs allow members to accrue in comparison to a corporation or a partnership/sole proprietorship. Personal assets are safeguarded by LLCs in the event of liabilities or bankruptcy. As mentioned before, when businesses do not register themselves as a particular entity, they are automatically considered a sole proprietorship or partnership, depending upon the number of people engaged in the business.

This means that the method of conversion of a partnership or a sole proprietorship will be the same as that of the registration of an LLC, as far as partnerships and sole proprietorships are concerned. The owner will have to check the website of the Secretary of State to determine the various procedures and forms that need to be filed. They will need to choose an available business name, register the articles of organization, and hire a registered agent in the state where they want to conduct their business. As mentioned in the relevant section, some states also require the LLC to announce itself in the form of a public notice. This is another need that needs to be fulfilled if the owner wants to convert the partnership or the sole proprietorship into an LLC. Hence, as far as sole proprietorships and partnerships are concerned, the method of conversion into an LLC simply does not exist. Such businesses will need to follow the same method that they followed for the registration of an LLC.

This logically means that the steps required to be followed for the conversion of a corporation into an LLC will be much more complex. Here, as corporations are a separate legal entity, a proper conversion into an LLC will have to take place. In the case of a sole proprietorship or a partnership, no actual registration needs to have taken place for them to exist. There are three ways in which another business entity can be converted into an LLC. It can be done via a statutory merger, a statutory acquisition, or, in certain cases, a non-statutory conversion. A statutory merger will involve the company merging with another LLC, and the resultant company is registered as a new LLC.

In a nutshell, a merger involves more than one party, while a conversion involves only one company. In the case of a merger, the resultant company needs to be registered as a new LLC, while in the case of a conversion, the company can be directly converted into an LLC by filing a form. The final way in which the business structure of a company can be changed is via an acquisition. Here, another party ends up taking control of the company, which can happen both voluntarily and involuntarily. The new owner might decide to register the company as an LLC. Of course, the most common way in which a company is converted into an LLC is through direct conversion. As previously mentioned, corporations have a rather complex method of conversion.

Depending on whether it is a C-corporation or an S-corporation that needs to be converted, there are three ways in which this is done:

Statutory Conversion:

Most states have a statute that allows a corporation to be converted into an LLC. The nature of the corporation plays a role in determining the taxation to which the company will be subjected under the new system. S-corporations have pass-through taxation, while C-corporations pay taxes at the corporate level.

While the new LLC can choose to be taxed in several ways, the following requirements need to be fulfilled in order to complete the conversion:

- The directors must approve and prepare a plan of conversion, which is then expected to be presented to the shareholders of the company.
- If the stockholders approve the conversion, the certificate of conversion can be filed on the Secretary of State 'website. There are a range of other documents and forms that might require filing as well, including the certificate of LLC formation.

A statutory conversion is the easiest and most inexpensive way of converting in most cases, as the state itself allows the conversion to happen. If there is no such statute, a statutory merger might need to be approved.

Statutory Merger:

A statutory merger will involve the filing of a certificate of merger by the company. This will be done after the creation and registration of a new LLC. The company will then get the merger plan approved by the board of directors, present it to the shareholders, and a voting session will be conducted. If the majority votes in favor of the merger, the two parties can then merge, and the resultant company will be registered as an LLC. Before the certificate of merger and other required documents are filed, the company will also need to get the stockholders to exchange their shares for member rights.

While a conversion statute is available in most states, those that do not allow such conversion will require a statutory merger to be filed. The merger agreement will stipulate the conditions of the new regime and determine how the member rights are distributed among the members. A statutory merger might also require the original company to be dissolved, which will require a separate form to be filled out on the Secretary of State website. Such a method of conversion is obviously more expensive as the creation of a new LLC needs to take place. Finally, the most complicated way in which a conversion can take place is via a non-statutory conversion.

Non-Statutory Conversion:

A non-statutory conversion means that a statute for the merger of companies is not applicable to the company. Under special circumstances, the company might choose to convert this way. However, it is the most expensive and complicated way in which a conversion takes place. Here, a new LLC will need to be formed and registered first and foremost. The method is like the previous one. However, in a statutory conversion, automatic transfers of assets, debts, and liabilities take place, and the company only needs to formally convert the shares into member rights.

In the case of a non-statutory conversion, different agreements dealing with the debts, assets, and liabilities of the original company will need to be formally transferred to the new LLC. This method will also invariably involve the dissolution of the original company, which means that along with all the steps followed for a statutory conversion, the formal transfer of all the assets, debts, and liabilities of the company will also need to take place. This makes a non-statutory conversion the most complicated and expensive method of conversion into an LLC.

CHAPTER 8: FORMING A REAL ESTATE LLC—A GUIDE

The real estate market is considered one of the safest industries to invest in. It is one of the oldest industries and has a huge potential for consistent profits. At the same time, the property market can be hit by a range of unpredictable factors that can drive down the value of an investment quickly. This means that a company that invests in real estate will want a certain level of protection for the personal assets of its owners. An LLC easily allows for that without affecting the amount of control that members have over their investments or the decision-making of the entity.

Moreover, real estate LLCs also give people the option of owning properties with other people, meaning that they offer a lot of control over ownership, investment, and management. A real estate LLC is also protected from double taxation, which has made them a common option in the US. Moreover, if there are multiple people involved in the LLC, all of them not only get protection for their personal assets but will also be in a better position financially and otherwise if investments go awry or if the LLC is subjected to lawsuits. A real estate LLC therefore gives a lot of financial and management flexibility, protects against double taxation, and allows multiple people to be involved in profit and loss sharing.

Like in most cases, the biggest reason why real estate investors tend to choose to register as an LLC is the personal protection that is afforded to them. In case of a loss, the debt or liability will be placed under the company's name, which means that the company will have a greater chance of continuing to exist. The members will also have a better chance of making up for bad investments and paying off their liabilities, an option that might not be available in the case of an individual investor in the form of a sole proprietorship.

Additionally, while real estate LLCs offer the same kind of tax benefits as other LLCs, most real estate companies tend to be involved in the business of managing rental property incomes as well. By simply managing rental property incomes, the LLC will be able to save 20% of the overall business income tax. Furthermore, the real estate market tends to be rigid in the sense that prices do not show huge deflections. By investing with partners via an LLC, members can easily demarcate the overall ownership according to the investment as well. Via the LLC operating agreement, members can split both ownership and profits according to their personal stake, which gives a higher degree of flexibility with respect to the distribution of profits.

Another derived advantage of choosing to invest in real estate as an LLC is that it gives the company a professional outlook, which is bound to benefit it in the real estate market. There is little doubt that real estate LLCs are ideal ways of investing in the real estate market, although there might be some minor downfalls. These include:

The Due on Sale Clause
When a real estate LLC acquires a property that was previously owned by an individual, changing the name of the owner might trigger a due-on-sale clause, which will mean that the loan amount might need to be immediately

paid. The property might then be foreclosed if the LLC cannot pay the loan amount immediately. This is a problem, especially when the owner was previously a member of the LLC. The member might need to talk to their lender or bank, or the lender of the previous owner, and request that they waive the clause. In most cases, this should not be a complicated process, as the lender will have no intention of impeding the sale of the property.

The Extra Cost

Just like with every LLC, there are various scenarios when personal liability is triggered, especially when a crime has been committed. In such a scenario, the LLC will not be able to protect the member. The extra costs and the requirements that need to be regularly fulfilled might prove to be a burden, especially if personal liability might still not be available, depending on the case. The cost can therefore be seen as a waste in some situations, especially if the company is doing well and is not potentially the subject of lawsuits.

It is obvious that, similar to medical practitioners, real estate investors can also derive a range of benefits from choosing to register as an LLC. The owners and investors are expected to do the necessary research and compare the kinds of benefits that they can accrue when compared with other business structures. A sole proprietor or a partnership will not have personal liability protection, while a corporation will subject the investor to double taxation and reduce their control over their investments and management. While the investor should research and understand what kind of benefits and profits, they can accrue by choosing to invest in real estate as an LLC, there is little doubt that there are certain special advantages that make LLCs the ideal option for real estate investors.

CHAPTER 9: THINGS TO THINK ABOUT WHEN STARTING AN LLC

With that, it will be fair to say that the previous chapters have succeeded in providing a detailed account of the entire journey that needs to be followed in order to create an LLC. Similar steps come into play when an existing business owner tries to convert their structure into an LLC. There are a range of basic and specific details and requirements that might need to be fulfilled when an LLC is formed.

While it might be crucial to understand the kinds of requirements, expectations, and advantages that converting into an LLC might entail, owners might be required to talk to an expert or a lawyer at different stages of the process. Furthermore, it might also be crucial to research the state in which the owner wants to start their LLC. For example, for foreign residents, Wyoming is said to be the ideal state, while for locals, Delaware is said to be the most common choice. This is due to various statutory, requirement-related, and other benefits that these states provide to LLCs, along with other benefits that might be applicable based on the industry and the scope of the company.

In most situations, state laws govern the kinds of decisions and requirements that need to be fulfilled by the LLC. For reference, owners must visit and research the website of the Secretary of State and keep a lookout for any other information that might help them grow or improve their business. Other basic points that need to be considered might be related to the name of the LLC.

Some states have specific requirements with respect to the name that need to be fulfilled by the members. For example, most states do not allow certain terms to be used that suggest that the LLC is related to some industries, such as insurance or banking. Another obvious limitation is that most states will not allow a business to choose a name that another business has already registered previously. Again, the Secretary of State website generally includes all such information related to the name of the company.

Moving on, most states also have certain requirements related to the registered agent. Apart from being over 18, the agent must be a resident of the state in which the LLC is being registered and oversee all communication that is directed towards the company. Some states have certain other requirements that need to be fulfilled, something that must also be checked on the Secretary of State website.

As far as the two most important documents related to the LLC are concerned, both the articles of organization and the operating agreement can easily be created nowadays. The articles of organization have specific formats and information that needs to be included, and most secretary of state websites have detailed guidelines and even proper formats. The same is true for operation agreements. A range of websites provide detailed formats and might even allow extensive customizations to be added. The operating agreement is the method via which members introduce customizations with respect to the LLC. The members must decide upon the various decision-making processes, powers, responsibilities, and all management-related information which must then be added to the operating agreement.

The operating agreement also acts as a tool to decide what kind of processes will take place if a member wants to leave or if the company ends up going bankrupt. The articles of organization, on the other hand, include basic details that need to be filed with the relevant state. Finally, other things that members need to be aware of are that there are a range of other information-related forms that need to be filed on the secretary of state's website. The website might also release notifications for LLCs related to specific requirements or reports that need to be submitted. For an LLC member, the Secretary of State website therefore becomes extremely important, as it includes all kinds of information and actions that the company needs to take in order to be in good standing with the government.

While comparisons between LLCs and other forms of business structures have been consistently made so far, the fact is that there are other forms of structures that might be more suitable for a particular company. Still, LLCs offer a range of hybrid features and have a wide scope that allows different kinds of businesses to exist as LLCs. While proper research will be required at every step of the way, the basic legal and other requirements should be the crux of the focus for senior members. Apart from those requirements, the LLC is only a business structure, and it is the overall health of the business that will determine its success or failure.

In this way, there is little doubt that LLCs can be the ideal business structure for a range of different companies. At the same time, speaking with a professional expert might not be the worst of ideas, especially the beginning.

CHAPTER 10: DO LLCS HAVE A GREATER CHANCE OF SUCCEEDING THAN OTHER STRUCTURES?

The question is meaningless in and of itself. It might be true that a large range of successful companies in recent years might be LLCs. However, the chosen business structure can only aid the success of a business, not create it. Whether the business is profitable will depend upon its health, resources, potential profit mechanisms, and a range of other predictable and unpredictable factors that form the market conditions.

The fact is that, like all businesses, LLCs are also subjected to the same kinds of business risks. While the structure can make the jobs of management, taxation, and personal liability protection easier and more straightforward, that does not guarantee the success of the overall business. Whether the business will be profitable depends upon a range of other factors related to the industry, the health, the management, and the profit-making potential of the company. Members need to accept the existence of this risk, which they need to undertake in order to have a chance of creating a successful business.

Furthermore, LLCs offer a higher level of protection for personal assets than partnerships or sole proprietorships. Apart from being an advantage due to the nature of certain industries, this protection does not mean that personal liability can never arise. If a crime is committed or a member commits fraud against other members, the member in question is personally liable, and any successful lawsuit will result in liability on the person. In such a situation, the LLC might even be safe, as the member might be guilty of a crime.

The other major advantage that LLCs provide is tax flexibility. Most corporations undergo double taxation, and LLCs have the option of being taxed like partnerships and sole proprietorships. Again, certain companies can save a large amount of taxes by converting into an LLC, another factor that needs to be well researched in advance. This means that a smart entrepreneur can identify the various advantages that converting into an LLC might provide them with. However, this does not mean that the business has a greater chance of succeeding. Rather, a potentially successful business might be easy to manage and grow for entrepreneurs if they opt for an LLC structure.

As mentioned previously, forming an LLC is the beginning of the journey, and a range of requirements, forms, and other formalities also need to be completed afterwards. There are a range of legal procedures that need to be followed, and specific forms need to be filed in order to structure the taxation system that the LLC will follow. In most situations, LLCs choose to be taxed like partnerships, and they are supposed to file Form 1065 for taxation purposes with the IRS.

Furthermore, various states also have other requirements. Every LLC needs to have a registered agent, while some states also stipulate the minimum number of employees that need to be hired. Other legal requirements are related to the demarcation of responsibilities. The articles of organization sometimes need to include information about the various responsibilities and departments of the company, as well as information about the heads. Hence, while LLCs have their own set of advantages, there are various formalities and requirements that need to be checked and completed on a regular basis.

This means that LLCs might have little to no influence over the success of the business. Rather, LLCs are simply the structure in which the business chooses to exist. The structure must obviously be chosen to maximize the chances of the business succeeding. However, whether the LLC structure can do that is another question that needs to be answered by the company itself. LLCs are hybrid structures that have outlined advantages that have been described in detail thus far. However, whether other structures can give the same kind of benefits is something that needs to be thought about. Corporations are sometimes better off with a different business structure simply due to the number of people involved. Hence, LLCs offer a business structure that is unique and combines the most important advantages of both corporations and partnerships. However, converting into an LLC does not guarantee success, and a range of different factors need to be considered before making the decision.

CHAPTER 11: MISTAKES TO AVOID WHILE FORMING LLC

As talked about before, real estate investors can acquire a range of benefits from choosing to operate as an LLC. Aside from tax advantages and asset protection, the real estate industry necessitates the acquisition of capital. A range of LLCs cannot acquire new assets simply because of their poor credit ratings. In such a scenario, individual members are sometimes forced to take out loans against their personal assets. However, forming an LLC will allow the business to build up credit, which will directly improve its lending power. This in turn will allow for quicker growth and the acquisition of assets, which can prove to be extremely useful especially towards the beginning of the LLC's formation.

Once the members are certain of their business structure, they can continue to improve the financial health of the LLC by improving its credit rating. A range of different benefits, especially in the case of government contracts, are available to LLCs that have better credit ratings than others. Of course, there are a range of mistakes that members are liable to commit when an LLC is being formed, especially towards the beginning of the journey. First and foremost, members sometimes tend to believe that their business is simply too small to be converted into an LLC.

However, in recent years, statistics prove that LLCs have become the ideal option for smaller businesses as well, and there is no reason to think that the trend will settle down anytime soon. The truth is that LLCs offer a variety of unique advantages that most businesses, particularly small businesses, do not have. Sole proprietors and partnerships, especially in the retail sector, often come up against bigger, more established companies.

In such a scenario, establishing a successful business can prove to be an even bigger challenge. Not only are the established companies financially secure and already have a good flow of profits, but the individual owners do not have a lot of personal liability attached unless they commit a crime. For a sole proprietorship, a smaller business, or a partnership, the playing field can be leveled to some extent by simply forming an LLC. Members of an LLC are bound to be more expensive in their plans and can register better growth when compared to the same business operating as a partnership.

Hence, rather than the size or the nature of the establishment, it is the benefits on offer that must be considered when choosing the business structure. There is no reason to believe that smaller businesses cannot function as LLCs. As the discourse until now has proved, there are a range of potential benefits, especially for certain industries, that can be accrued via LLC formation.

Secondly, another thing to consider is the state in which the LLC is registered. As mentioned, several times, each state has its own set of rules and regulations that apply to the formation and upkeep of LLCs. Certain states have provisions for foreign LLCs, while others might have more complicated provisions that can be minor hindrances. Hence, owners should also research the various laws and regulations, as well as the formalities and requirements they will need to fulfill in order to form an LLC in the state of their choosing. Furthermore, while LLCs do offer a sense of protection for personal assets, that is only true until an act is committed that attracts personal liability.

Members must be mindful and aware of the extent and limited nature of the protection that is available to them as far as an LLC is concerned. Hence, while LLCs can prove to be ideal, members should research and consult an expert to understand the extent of benefits that they may be able to accrue from different business structures. There are bound to be certain provisions and requirements that owners end up missing. Having an expert ensures that the LLC is properly run and does not face any legal or other kind of trouble in the future.

Once the LLC is formed and registered and all other formalities have been completed, the business will be able to function properly. However, most states issue regular notices that inform LLCs of new requirements that need to be fulfilled. The Secretary of State website can prove to be extremely useful for staying updated with respect to any changing provisions that might be applicable to the company as well.

This means that even after the LLC has been formed, regularly keeping track of the relevant state website can also prove to be crucial. This will help the company stay compliant with any requirements and stay updated on any information that it must know about or respond to. Another common misconception that owners tend to have been that the LLC registration acts as a business license for the company. However, that is not true, and the relevant licenses still need to be bought by the company. The registration of the LLC only ensures that the state recognizes the company as a separate legal entity.

Finally, other factors that might need consideration are related to the filing of forms and the reluctance of owners to get help from experts. Getting the right advice can help owners recognize issues even before they arise and be proactive in ensuring that the company does not run into unpredictable problems. As far as the filing of various forms is concerned, members need to ensure that any templates that they download and use for the articles of organization or the operating agreement follow all the norms, include the relevant information that is required by the state, and have all the relevant provisions and customizations that the members wish to add. Ensuring the above should prove enough in most situations and help members register, run, and grow their LLCs to the best of their abilities.

Chapter 12: Recommendations and Takeaways

As the writeup comes closer to its conclusion, there are a range of key takeaways that entrepreneurs need to know and understand about the LLC business structure. While the concept was created so as to combine the best features of the two most common business structures, LLCs provide a level of versatility that can prove extremely beneficial to various businesses. Smaller businesses that are still in the developmental stage often find themselves staring at markets that are dominated by bigger companies.

The risk of potential losses can be devastating, especially as these companies generally do not have owners with deep pockets. Irrespective of the quality of the business, its application, and the decision-making of entrepreneurs, businesses can register losses in a variety of ways. With corporations, bigger companies generally have protection for the personal assets of the owners. This means that unless they are involved in wrongdoing, their personal assets are safe and will not be exposed when lawsuits against the company are filed.

For smaller companies, this protection proves to be a significant advantage, but the complicated nature and management-related rigidity of corporations make them problematic for a range of reasons. Quite a few of these companies might not even have 10 employees and simply do not need the management structure that a corporation lends. On the other hand, corporations are exposed to double taxation. This is something sole proprietors and partnerships do not undergo.

While doing business as a sole proprietorship or a partnership is straightforward, companies that are looking to grow in the future need a management structure without being exposed to extra taxes. In this way, LLCs are a solution for smaller entrepreneurs to have a level playing field and allow them to compete against bigger companies. Of course, there are a range of basic recommendations that should be followed in most cases.

First and foremost, the business name of the company not only acts as an identity for customers and the overall competition, but there are also various requirements that need to be fulfilled. Business owners should be careful with the names they choose and ensure that they are willing to stick with the name in the future as well. For foreign LLCs, having a dependable registered agent proves paramount. There are various times when urgent communication needs to be passed on to the owners.

The registered agent should have a proper schedule, be easily reachable, and be quick in delivering communications to company owners. At times, the registered agent may need to meet with various parties in order to handle matters on the company's behalf. This means that the agent must be properly registered and should have a good track record.

Moving on, there are various things that can only be taken care of by the owners. For example, the procedures that go behind the registration of the LLC and the articles of organization need to be studied and researched well. There are generally multiple ways of converting a company into an LLC, as mentioned before. The owners must be willing to put in the time and figure out the best method that is available to them.

A statutory conversion tends to be the most inexpensive and uncomplicated way of converting a company into an LLC. Furthermore, every state requires a range of documents to be filed. The Secretary of State website generally includes all information regarding the formalities that the owners need to fulfill. The owners therefore need to stay updated and ensure that their LLCs are in good standing with the state. This will ensure that no issues come up if and when there are matters pertaining to the state.

Apart from the articles of organization, the operating agreement also plays an important role and enables a range of important customizations that owners might need. State laws generally have rigid guidelines that need to be followed if the operating agreement does not state these customizations. Hence, the kind of operating agreement, various provisions related to the future and unforeseen situations, and other customizations must all be added. The operating agreement also needs to be filed correctly and must have a proper, well-researched format.

Once the members ensure that the above is being taken care of to the required extent, they can then focus on the business itself and its growth. Keeping the company active and profitable will require a lot of work and determination. Owners will need to ensure that they have the right resources and manpower to ensure that all these tasks are completed on time.

Of course, there are things to remember and heed as well. LLCs offer a limited amount of personal liability protection, which means that any wrongdoing will attract personal liability, even if the company is sued instead. LLCs are easier to manage and more straightforward than most corporations because there is less paperwork involved.

With the level of flexibility in ownership and management that LLCs lend, the aim is simple. LLCs have been created to level the playing field for smaller companies and allow them to compete on the same footing. LLCs also offer a high amount of flexibility with respect to profit distribution, which is just another way in which a business owner can make use of the business structure.

CONCLUSION

Needless to say, there are a number of reasons why LLCs have become increasingly popular in the US in recent years. The advantages that they lend over other business structures allow companies to accrue the best features without necessarily wasting the same amount of time on management and registration-related purposes. This allows members to focus on the most important part of the business: its functioning.

The idea is to enable smaller companies to be bolder with their approach. Businesses tend to not go "all out," especially in the initial stages, because quite a bit of seeding is required to generate profits. With limited budgets, companies often find themselves unable to fairly compete with established corporations. However, corporations in themselves have tangible benefits and various disadvantages.

With an LLC, an owner can accrue these advantages, refuse the disadvantages, and get a large amount of management-related flexibility that is generally associated with partnerships or sole proprietorships. Smaller businesses, partnerships, and sole proprietorships can also benefit from converting into an LLC. This is in the form of the taxation-related advantages. With an LLC, owners can choose to be taxed in multiple ways. This ensures that they can generate a high level of customization with respect to their business structure and find ways to succeed that might even be considered non-traditional in certain industries.

Regardless, as mentioned before, some of the biggest companies in the world have also been functioning as LLCs. There is little doubt that LLCs can prove to be the ideal business structure for a range of businesses, irrespective of their size. With that, readers have all the information they need related to the functioning, formation and registration of an LLC. While LLCs can make the job easier and allow owners to make use of different kinds of provisions, the business structure only affects the fate of the business to a limited extent.

Rather than the structure, it is the overall idea, scope for profits, and the work put in that determine whether the business will prove to be a success or not. For entrepreneurs looking to have maximum control over their company, its profits, and its management, LLCs seem to be the ideal choice. Because entrepreneurs frequently have limited resources, converting to an LLC can sometimes be the deciding factor.

For example, a company starving for money is bound to benefit from the lack of double taxation and will stay afloat for a few more weeks or months. Some of the biggest businesses underwent long periods of stagnation before booming into successful empires. Quite a few of the biggest companies and their owners also had good luck on their sides.

Mark Zuckerberg's Facebook, now known as Meta, had a huge ownership-related controversy in the early years of its inception. Companies like Twitter and other popular social media platforms benefited from the timing as well as their ability to stay up to date and in touch with their audiences. There is little doubt that there is no correct way of succeeding. While that is true in life itself, it seems especially true with entrepreneurs, considering the unorthodox way in which some of the biggest company owners run their businesses.

Elon Musk, for example, has forced a mass exodus of employees from Twitter ever since he took over the company. (Twitter Sacks "Roughly 50%" of Staff; Elon Musk Says, "No Choice When...," n.d.) Musk has forced roughly 50% of employees out of the company, which is bound to drive up profits in the coming time for the company. While the method might not be "ideal," big decisions sometimes need to be taken in order to ensure success.

For a business, there are a range of important decisions that the members will have to take at different points in time. During these moments, rather than the business structure that was chosen, it is the entrepreneur who will be responsible for the decisions the company takes. With an LLC, owners can make these decisions quickly and have detailed guidelines set in place in the event of various special incidents. Hence, while converting the company into an LLC will help, it will have little to no influence on whether the overall business can evolve into a successful one. As talked about in the writeup throughout, there are a range of things that owners need to consider and know when forming an LLC.

From the potential advantages to the disadvantages, the owners must be aware of the consequences and understand the various ways in which forming an LLC can help them. The current writeup acts as a guidebook of sorts. It presents all the information required by owners in order to form an LLC, as well as the various features that the structure lends to the business. Once members have decided that converting into an LLC will be beneficial, they need to research the procedure and understand the various costs that they might have to incur due to this conversion.

While some differences with respect to various states exist, the overall idea is the same. LLCs have been created with the intention of allowing smaller businesses to protect themselves from personal liability without sacrificing the kind of control they have over their company. While the timing and size of the business are important factors to consider, LLCs generally do better than harm to a business. When combined with passion, drive, and the urge to grow consistently, every business can be converted into a highly successful one!

REFERENCES

Hayes, A. (n.d.). *Understanding LLC Operating Agreements.* Investopedia. https://www.investopedia.com/terms/l/llc-operating-agreement.asp

Hussain, A. (2022, September 13). *Understanding Articles of Organization.* Investopedia. https://www.investopedia.com/terms/a/articles-of-organization.asp

IRS. (2019). *Limited Liability Company LLC | Internal Revenue Service.* Irs.gov. https://www.irs.gov/businesses/small-businesses-self-employed/limited-liability-company-llc

Is it Time to Think About an LLC for Your Business? | Fitzpatrick Lentz & Bubba. (n.d.). Www.flblaw.com. Retrieved November 21, 2022, from https://www.flblaw.com/is-it-time-to-think-about-an-llc-for-your-business/

Kenton, W. (2021, August 22). *The Truth About Limited Liability Companies.* Investopedia. https://www.investopedia.com/terms/l/llc.asp

Limited Liability Company Act, Revised - Uniform Law Commission. (n.d.). Www.uniformlaws.org. https://www.uniformlaws.org/committees/community-home?CommunityKey=bbea059c-6853-4f45-b69b-7ca2e49cf740

Prakash, P. (2020, October 30). *How LLCs Pay Taxes.* NerdWallet.

https://www.nerdwallet.com/article/small-business/small-business-llc-taxes

SOI Tax Stats - *Partnership Statistics by Entity Type* | Internal Revenue Service. (n.d.). Www.irs.gov. Retrieved November 21, 2022, from https://www.irs.gov/statistics/soi-tax-stats-partnership-statistics-by-entity-type

The four best states to start an LLC in 2023 | doola blog. (n.d.). Www.doola.com. Retrieved December 6, 2022, from https://www.doola.com/blog/best-state-to-start-an-llc

Twitter Sacks Roughly 50%" Of Staff, Elon Musk Says No Choice When..." (n.d.). NDTV.com. https://www.ndtv.com/world-news/twitter-sacks-roughly-50-percent-of-staff-as-elon-musk-launches-overhaul-3492020